Bridge by Bridge
through London

Written and Illustrated
by Tony Waters
Edited by Elizabeth Tonge

D1563222

THE THAMES FROM TOWER BRIDGE TO TEDDINGTON

Pryor Publications

British Library Cataloguing in Publication Data
Waters, Tony, 1920-
Bridge by Bridge through London:
the Thames from Tower to Teddington
1. London Thames River
I. Title
914.21

ISBN 0-946140-6-X

© Pryor Publications 1989

75 Dargate Road, Yorkletts
Whitstable, Kent CT5 3AE

Typeset in Palatino Medium by
Proset Photocomp Limited, Canterbury
Printed and bound by
Whitstable Litho Printers, Whitstable

Contents

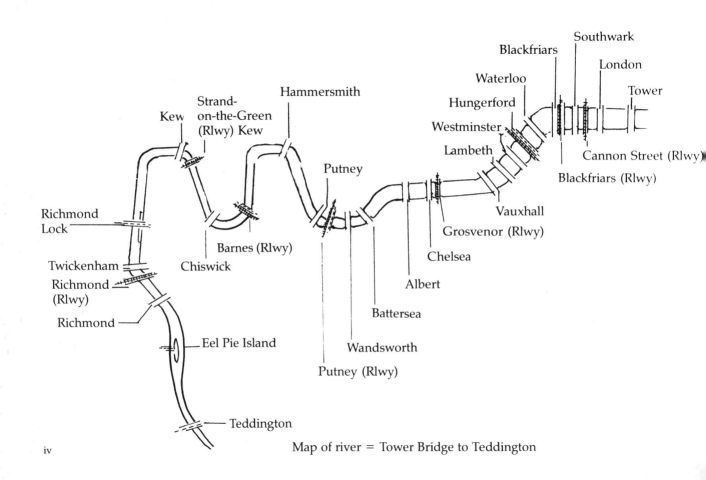

Map of river = Tower Bridge to Teddington

iv

INTRODUCTION

A great river has many aspects. A nation's history can be traced along its course; it can be the means by which a country's commerce and wealth flourishes; it is a flowing highway giving work or pleasure to those who travel or sport upon its surface and a source of quiet enjoyment to all who just stand and admire its undoubted beauty. It is a natural boundary between territories, a barrier to be crossed.

To cross by ferry boat is a particular pleasure which is the only means of crossing some rivers. Wherever it is possible to build a bridge, the advantage that it has over a ferry in terms of convenience is obvious. Tunnels may be equally convenient but add nothing to the river scene, whereas a bridge in most instances enhances it.

The River Thames has a traceable history of bridge-crossing that is about 2000 years old, the first known bridge being built by the occupying Romans. This book traces a journey through London following the river's course, looking at each bridge passed on the way and, where appropriate, at the interesting things that surround it. The journey begins at the first bridge on the Thames, and ends at the top of the tideway at Teddington Locks.

Although it covers a distance of only about twenty-four miles, a small section of the river's two hundred and five miles course, it is not a quick journey, for there is much of interest to delay the traveller.

Across the tideway are stretched eighteen road bridges, nine railway bridges and six foot-bridges, three of which are incorporated in railway bridges. No two bridges are the same and each adds its own charm and interest to the scene. What better place could be found from which to observe a river than from the middle of a bridge?

Tony Waters

TOWER BRIDGE

When I was a boy, my mother had many fascinating tales of her father's engineering days. Some were very amusing, particularly those of things that did not go quite as planned; others could be dramatic, of dangers and difficulties overcome. I enjoyed them all, and their countless retellings.

Grandfather was an engineer working in steel and large machinery installations. I heard stories of road-rail bridges, built over raging water in Scotland; of the building and dismantling of the Great Wheel at the now forgotten Earls Court pleasure ground; and of how grandfather built the famous Tower Bridge, an undertaking viewed by mother with great pride.

As she told it, I conjured up a vision of a Goliath grandfather spanning the river Thames with the remarkable Tower Bridge, entirely by his own unaided efforts. I visualised a kind of enormous building set of steel struts and grandfather busy screwing it together with massive nuts and bolts. At school I enjoyed a measure of one-upmanship in actually knowing somebody who had been concerned in the building of such a famous bridge. I was very proud of my remote association with it. Mechanical marvels in those days certainly ranked equal with the electronic wonders that occupy the attention of today's youth.

As a child I remember seeing a tall, grey, upright figure, solemn, austere and rather forbidding but recognised by me as grandfather. Had I been as a child of today, I might have grabbed hold of his hand and asked him if he had ever built a space ship. As he has long passed on to wherever bridge builders go when they have done with spanning the rivers of this world, I can never know whether this would have pleased him or not. I do know that it was from my grandfather's connection with bridges that my interest in the river stemmed.

Inevitably, changes have been made in updating the power system of the bridge. Today's visitors can inspect the engine room which once housed the steam engines; the latter have been replaced with electric motors, and an oil hydraulic system has taken the place of the original water system.

Whenever I have had the pleasure of showing visitors round London, the Tower of London and of course Tower Bridge have been high on my list of places to visit. On the rare occasions when the wide roadway has opened up while my visitors stood gaping in astonishment, I have been apt to say proudly "my grandfather built that", ignoring the fact that he was only one of many who contributed various skills to the work.

Grandfather's official position was that of overseer, which in today's terminology would make him a sort of site agent or some such relatively lowly rank in the Tower Bridge building project. So far as I am concerned, however, he built it.

The original steam engines, with an energy of over 350 horsepower, were housed in the base of the gate tower on the south side of the bridge. Together with their associated water hydraulic system they were capable of raising the road bascules from the horizontal to the vertical position in 90 seconds. This made it theoretically possible for a ship to pass through in about four minutes. It usually took longer.

In practice, the bascules were not usually raised to the full vertical. They were so raised as a salute to a visiting ship of special importance, such as one carrying a royal visitor or other foreign state dignitary, or if a ship of unusually large size wished to pass through.

Four minutes of road traffic stand-still was enough to cause bad congestion even in the days of horse-drawn vehicles. At any time when needed during the day or night, the bridge would be raised. Today if the bridge were raised just once during the times of traffic rush hour, the effect would be felt for miles around on both sides of the river. For a ship to pass from the down stream — or lower pool, as that part of the river near Tower Bridge is called — to the up-stream or upper pool side, it was not always a simple matter of passing one ship through. There could be two or three arriving on a favourable tide and their passage could be complicated by other ships waiting to go down-stream on their way to the estuary. This greatly extended the time that the bridge remained open.

Thoughtfully, the means was provided to pedestrians of avoiding delays of possibly ten minutes or more, by the provision of walk-ways at high level. Stairways in the Towers lead up to the walks which link the Towers on opposite sides of the river, high above the roadway. Those people with the energy and the urgency could climb the 140 feet height of the stairs, pass over the open bascules and tramp down the other side. The effort involved in this exercise made it unattractive to most people, who preferred to wait and watch the ships pass through. Because the high level walks were under-used by the general public going normally about its business, but over-used by suicides, they were eventually closed.

However, the value of the walk-ways as view points, and therefore a popular tourist attraction, has been recognised. Now partly enclosed in glass, they have been re-opened and become attractive to a great many visitors, who do not seem to mind paying a fee to be allowed to climb the stairs for the benefit of what has been described as "the best view of London by the Thames".

Providing a footway was not the only purpose of the high level links between the towers. Indeed, that was probably a secondary purpose. Apart from bracing the two towers across the space between them, they also served to carry the pipes of the original water hydraulic system. Viewed from the river, the bridge towers appear to rise in stone from bases on the stone cutwaters that support them. In fact, they are steel structures covered with stone. It was the steel work and the installation of the engines that operated the bridge with which my grandfather was concerned.

We tend to think of the conscious need to care for the environment as a purely present-day concern, but in Tower Bridge we have a fine example of Victorian awareness of this consideration. The approving authority insisted that, because of its close proximity to the Tower of London, the structure of the bridge must be visually appropriate to the area.

Two men were involved in the accepted design. Sir John Woolf-Barry was the engineer who designed the steel work and Sir Horace Jones was responsible for the stone cladding. The neo-Gothic result may not be to the liking of some people, but what style would please everybody? I have never met anybody who was concerned to change Tower Bridge; it has become as much part of the scene as the historic Tower of London.

One day, perhaps, a cross-river route will be devised for road traffic so that it need not cross the bridge and then it might be possible for the opening of the bridge to be operated on a regular programme — say twice a day. It would, I am sure, draw crowds of visitors to watch it, just as does the changing of the guard in Whitehall. There is an unused tunnel under the river that crosses close to the line of Tower Bridge and was originally intended for use as a railway route; could this, I sometimes wonder, be adapted to take road traffic?

There would be no problem nowadays in opening the bridge. When steam provided the power and the bascules were raised at any time of the day or night as required, a considerable crew had to be available to man it on a shift basis. It required 80 men and a superintendent engineer. Today, electric power and hydraulic system have made such a crew unnecessary. A two-man crew is normally on duty, one of whom is there as a safety precaution against a one-man failure.

An incident occurred a few years ago which shows that such precautions are wise. Preparations for raising the bridge include a stopping of all traffic

TOWER BRIDGE

YATES

approaching it, and the clearance of all vehicles and pedestrians from it. Never should it be possible for any traffic to enter the bridge once the bascules are ready for lifting. One afternoon, however, a double-decker London bus approached the bridge and by some fault was allowed to pass under the tower arch and on to the roadway just as the bridge was starting to open. The driver of the bus was faced with the dilema of whether to attempt to stop, with the risk of falling into the river if he failed; or to attempt to rush his bus over the slowly increasing gap. He chose the latter course, stamped on his accelerator and the bus surged forward. It leapt the gap with a considerable bump but nobody was really hurt and the bus apparently suffered no obvious damage. It was a near thing and fortunate that the bus was travelling along that side of the bridge that rises just ahead of the other side which it slightly overlaps in closing. Had it been the other way round the result might have been disastrous for both the bus and the passengers.

Most visitors to London are aware that the Tower of London and Tower Bridge have much to offer. What is not so well known are the other attractions of the area.

The Tower of London stands on naturally rising ground overlooking the river; viewed from the South Bank, tower and bridge make a most satisfying picture. Looking up or down river, and at St Katharine's dock which adjoins the bridge on the downstream side, there is excellent scope for photography or sketching.

St Katharine's dock was built to allow certain cargoes to be brought as close as possible to the City of London warehouses. Despite a great deal of public protest at the time, the dock basin was dug out from a site on which the principle building was St Katharine's church, from which the dock took its name.

Around it there rose a group of dockside warehouses of elegant character, the most notable being the Ivory House, which fortunately escaped wartime damage. In its day, it held fabulous values of ivory; indeed, most of the ivory coming into the country came through St Katharine's dock. The Ivory House is a spendidly proportioned building of mellow brick with graceful arches at wharfside level. It is set back from the water's edge with the upper floors projecting, so that cargoes could be hauled straight up from ships' holds without obstructing wharfside activity.

Adjoining buildings, many of which were destroyed during the war, appropriately complemented the Ivory House and housed special cargoes. There was an indigo house, which handled the import of indigo used by the textile dyeing industry. Surprisingly, there was a flower house importing cargoes of flowers from which perfume was extracted at a distillery within the dock area. Many grocery staple foods such as tea and dried fruit also came to St Katharine's. These commodities and raw materials were marketed or supplied to industry by the business houses of the nearby City of London.

Wartime damage, however, caused businesses to move away; in any case, although it was well enough suited to take relatively small ships, the dock was not big enough, being only about five acres, for use by the larger post-war vessels. Gradually, shipping was drawn away from London by the opening of dock facilities lower down river in deeper water.

Trade at St Katharine's dock officially closed in 1969. Many discussions were held about its future. The architectural merit of the Ivory House ensured that in the re-development plans which were eventually adopted, it became the centre around which everything else was arranged. It is now a building of high-class residential accommodation. A new hotel replaces some of the old buildings on one side, and shops and restaurants have been opened in the wharfside level of old warehouses. Where sail and steam vessels once tied up there is now a colourful marina. In one part of the dock, restored Thames and Medway barges are moored, and elsewhere a number of old ships can be visited for a moderate entrance fee. Access to all other public parts of the dock is free.

There is much else of interest to delight visitors — for instance, the beautiful "dolphin and girl" statue by David Wynne which stands on the riverside with Tower Bridge in the background. From one particular point of view, which I am sure photographers will delight in finding, it appears that the girl is diving off the bridge towards the rising dolphin.

St Katharine's dock can be entered from the north end of the bridge down steps which lead to the riverside walk. The walk also passes under Tower Bridge and gives access to the passenger-boat landing-stage, crossing the point of entry to the notorious Traitors' Gate of the Tower of London.

Up river from here one can see HMS Belfast, silhouetted against the second bridge on the Thames — London Bridge.

LONDON BRIDGE

The short way to London Bridge is to walk by the Tower of London and continue along Tower Hill to Lower Thames Street, on past the old Billingsgate market building which once housed London's fish market. Ahead can be seen the mass of London Bridge, and to the right, the Monument, commemorating the great fire of London of 1666, standing at the cross road of Monument Street and Fish Street.

"London Bridge is falling down, falling down, falling down," goes the old nursery rhyme, but which London Bridge?

There have been many, dating back to the time of the Roman occupation. For centuries London was the only place on the Thames where there was a bridge, and all the earlier bridges suffered problems of stability or disasters making their replacement necessary. The present bridge replaced the famous one designed by John Rennie.

In the 1960s I saw evidence that the Rennie bridge was indeed starting the process of falling down. Cruising up-stream against an ebb tide on a pleasure boat, I noticed indications that were quite clear. A wet line on the masonry left by the receding water, when compared to joints between stones, showed that the bridge was leaning away from its centre. How long, I wondered, before this bridge too, starts falling down?

There is little detail available of a Roman bridge that is said to have crossed the river at this point. As there was a settlement on the north side, on the hill that shaped the river's course, and a smaller one on the south side which was fringed with wide marsh, there must have been a link between the two that was more than a ferry boat. It was probably a timber structure with perhaps some pontoon sections.

There is some record of the existence of a bridge in about the year 980, when the Viking King Olaf is said to have sailed up the Thames and set fire to a bridge and the surrounding buildings, in what appears to have been an act of general plunder. Some historians say that Olaf destroyed the bridge by having ropes tied between its supporting posts and his boats, then ordering his crews to row with the tide until the bridge collapsed. Perhaps he employed both fire and crew power to make sure of doing a good job. In south London, near the bridge, there is a district known as St Olav's, which is a reminder of the Viking invasion.

Almost everybody who could sail seems to have invaded Britain in those early centuries, the evidence being along the river banks. The Danes went well beyond London leaving signs of their intrusion in the upper Thames area. The Normans added their enduring mark to that left by the Romans, and Saxon remains abound.

Plenty of material was provided for the London Bridge nursery rhyme by the bridges that succeeded the one destroyed by the Vikings, the first three of which were all unstable.

In 1090 a great gale swept away a wooden bridge as well as destroying many buildings. As this was then the only point of bridge crossing a new one was built without delay. Sadly, it was destroyed by fire in 1135. With commendable persistence but perhaps without enough care, another bridge was built which became so unsafe that it was once more rebuilt in 1160. Had the nursery rhyme been composed by then, I wonder? Around 1170, the bridge was once more declared to be not only unsafe but dangerous.

Confidence in the use of timber having doubtless been shaken, the authorities decided to use stone for the next bridge. It took several years of deliberation to arrive at that decision, and the work was started in 1176.

When this bridge was built, the river was much wider than it is today; although some straightening of the river banks had been carried out, the present embankmenting was not done until the 19th century. The line of London's first stone bridge was about a hundred yards downstream from the present one, the south end being beside a church that still stands to mark the spot.

One of the problems which faces bridge builders on a strong tidal river like the Thames is the considerable scouring action of the fast moving currents, and this is as much a consideration with the heavier bridges of today as it was with the earlier relatively light constructions. Water scour and a deep clay base were the root causes of bridge instability.

When the first stone London Bridge was built, the many piers supporting the arches were protected by massive timber grids called starlings, to break the flow of the water. This they certainly did, but they also had the effect of channelling the water through the arches, causing it to become a fierce torrent.

Navigation through the bridge was difficult and dangerous. In spite of a drawbridge section in the wider middle arch to allow the passage of ships, many ships and rowed boats failed to ride the rushing water and were wrecked. Some watermen, as the ferryboat men were called, refused to attempt the "shooting" of the bridge at unfavourable states of tide. If the waterman was willing the passengers may not have been and they were often put ashore to walk past the hazard and then rejoin the boat on the other side. Despite the dangers of the trip, boatmen competed aggressively for the trade of passengers courageous enough to risk the shooting of the bridge.

The first stone bridge survived well into the 19th century, much longer than any of its predecessors. It was wider than they had been, and it was not long before buildings were erected upon it. Only a drawbridge in the middle prevented it from becoming occupied along its total length, on both sides, by some kind of building. Most of these buildings were shops and stores, some of which overlapped the parapets; there was also a chapel with access from the river by steps, and a gateway at each end on which were mounted spikes, for the gruesome purpose of displaying the heads of executed felons. So crowded with buildings and market stalls did the bridge become that it was only with difficulty that a horse-drawn cart could make its way across.

At one time, an engineer negotiated rights to use arches close to the north bank to install water wheels for the purpose of pumping water to the city, as far up as Holborn. I understand that his lease is still valid and that his successors still draw payment from the present-day water authority, in compensation for loss of rights when the bridge was demolished. This most successful of London bridges, which showed no sign of falling down, but simply became inadequate to cope with increasing traffic, was replaced with one of more graceful design made by John

Rennie in 1831.

Rennie's design, however, could not withstand the river scour as its predecessor had done, and the old problem developed, causing it to tend to incline to one side.

Quite apart from its obvious tilt, it became necessary to replace Rennie's bridge to accommodate the increasing volume of traffic in the post-war years. Its road width had already been increased by incorporating the width of the original footpaths and building other footpaths outwards, over the original sides.

An American developer, learning of the city's intention to build a new bridge, made an offer for the standing one. That he had no water for it to cross, worried him not one jot. It was just what he wanted for a new leisure park being laid out near Havasu City, Arizona.

The City of London authorities were no doubt delighted and probably not a little surprised to find that they had a customer for their old bridge. They were helped in the work of demolition by the collaboration of American engineers in devising a method of numbering and coding some 10,000 pieces of stone, each to be placed in its correct position when they reached Havasu. This great jigsaw puzzle was reassembled on dry land later and had water diverted under it. So the London Bridge of

London Bridge

WATERS

Victorian times survives in a pleasure park in Arizona, basking in such sunshine as was never expected to warm its old stones. A malicious little joke went round London at the time, that the Americans thought that they were buying Tower Bridge when they made their offer. I do not think that American developers are so naive, and as their engineers were in consultation with their London counterparts at every stage, it is clear that they knew exactly what they were buying.

It was an imaginative and ingenious scheme by the American developers and a compliment to Britain that they should have chosen one of its old relics to grace their splendid new park.

The scheme for dismantling the old bridge and building a wider one in its place, without serious disruption to traffic, called for an equally ingenious plan. To achieve this, an enormous structure of steel tubes rose high above the old bridge, occupying half its width. Traffic became two way on the other half and inasmuch as the tubular structure supported the work from above, a section of the bridge could be said to have been hung from it. First one side was dismantled and the new section constructed, and traffic realigned. Then the opposite side was treated in the same way and eventually the supporting tubes disappeared and the new wide bridge came into use.

The fact that it can now deliver more traffic each hour to London's city streets than they can adequately cope with, is a problem of quite a different nature.

Without a doubt, the builders of the new London Bridge can take pride in their skill in carrying out the work with no more disruption to road traffic than the closure of the bridge at some weekends. Nor has it disturbed the historically rich areas at each end of London Bridge.

On the south side of the bridge is the very busy commuter station named London Bridge Station. Thousands of people leave their trains at this station daily and walk across the river to the city. Some do this because of the convenience of its location to their place of work; some see it as welcome exercise after their suburban train journey; others do it just for the benefit of enjoying the river views.

So many do this daily trek across the bridge that during the rush hour the pavement disappears under the solid marching phalanx of brief case- and umbrella-carrying office workers.

There are many things of interest on both sides of the bridge and it would be easy to wander away from the river in pursuit of them. I will confine myself to those things that are close to the river.

On the north side just down a short hill of a street

on the right hand side, approaching the city, stands The Monument, designed by Sir Christopher Wren to commemorate the great fire of 1666, which almost destroyed the city. The height of the column is said to equal the distance from that spot to where the fire started. At the top there is a viewing gallery which can be reached by steep stairs. If you make it to the top you will be rewarded by superb views of the city and the river.

You can reach the centre of the city by following the road that leads directly from the bridge, which will bring you to the Mansion House, official residence of the Lord Mayor of London, the Royal Exchange, almost rubbing shoulders with the Bank of England, and St Paul's Cathedral.

The south side of the bridge is in another city, the City of Southwark. It is a part of London in which Charles Dickens set the scenes of some of his novels. If you walk over the bridge on the right hand side, going away from the London City, you will pass the spot where the bridge joins the bank which was the scene in "Oliver Twist" of Nancy's murder by Bill Sykes.

Looking up the river, you will see the railway bridge that serves Cannon Street railway terminus, marked by two attractive small towers which were retained when the old terminus was redeveloped.

Walk under the railway bridge that spans the road ahead and turn right just after you are clear of it and you will find yourself in "The Borough" fruit and produce market behind which is Southwark Cathedral.

The Cathedral is worth a visit; there is a lot of colour and activity about the market from the morning's early hours, but it all quietens down about midday, deserted by its salesmen and porters.

If, after visiting the Cathedral, you retrace your steps to cross the market and walk down the winding Park Street, you will come again to the river at Bankside and to the Anchor public house. In the entrance to the bars there stands a model of Shakespeare's Globe Theatre.

The Globe Theatre was built on a site just a little way along the narrow Bankside, a road that follows the river, but there were other theatres there also in Shakespeare's day, the best known of which was The Swan. Other places catering for Elizabethan public taste in entertainment, such as cock-fighting and bear-baiting, were also located near the theatres.

Sir Christopher Wren occupied a cottage, facing the river, which is identified by a plaque on the wall. When his masterpiece, St Paul's Cathedral, was being built on the opposite side of the river, he could watch its progress from his cottage. You can see for yourself, in spite of the buildings that have grown up between the Cathedral and the river bank, that he must have had a very good view.

If you walk back again past the Anchor you will see on the left a rather dingy narrow street of tall warehouses. It was in this street, named Clink Street, that the infamous debtors' prison was built and from which springs the warning to spendthrifts — "if you are not careful you will end up in the clink".

Film producers seeking a Victorian period background for a film have on more than one occasion used this area for its setting. Almost overnight, with the introduction of appropriate furnishings, costumes and props, the narrow streets have easily slipped back, visually, more than a hundred years.

Continue walking back to the main road, the Borough High Street, turn right, and not much more than a hundred yards along on the left-hand side there are large green wooden gates which are the entrance to a railway goods loading dock. However, although the gates obviously belong to British Rail, they carry a sign above them announcing "The George", and they lead also to the only Dickensian galleried inn now left in London.

The inn is not exactly as it was in Dickens's day; only part of the gallery now exists, on one side of what was then the courtyard. Furnishings in the

public bar have been kept much as they were, to preserve the Dickensian atmosphere, and there is a black-faced Parliament clock. Its large dial could be seen from outside through the windows; in the days when clocks were thought by Parliament to be a suitable subject for taxation, poor people could not afford clocks and depended on such privately provided timepieces to keep track of time.

A short distance from the entrance to the George, a church stands prominently on an island surrounded by traffic. This too has associations with Charles Dickens; it features in one of his finest novels and is known as "the Little Dorrit church".

SOUTHWARK BRIDGE

Upstream from London Bridge the view of the next road crossing, Southwark Bridge, is obscured by the first of several railway bridges, a number of which are of similar heavy, unlovely designs mainly or entirely of steel or iron.

In the case of this particular bridge, which carries rail traffic across the river from London Bridge station to the Southern Railway Cannon Street terminus on the city side, there is one feature that relieves its otherwise grey dullness. At its connection with the railway entrance to Cannon Street station, small spired towers surmount high mellow brick walls. They are much admired and photographed for their form, and were fortunately preserved when the terminus station underwent reconstruction.

Rival railway companies of the past built these bridges in a period of strong competition, when prestige, if nothing else, apparently demanded a terminus on the city side of the river.

Southwark Bridge was built to provide an alternative crossing of the river when London Bridge had become hopelessly congested. It was the building of a bridge at Southwark, resulting in diminished revenue from tolls to London Bridge, that led to the clearance of buildings which had been the original cause of the congestion of London Bridge and its approaches. The bridge now at Southwark replaced an earlier bridge, which had been built by a private company as a toll bridge and had been expected to be a profitable enterprise.

It failed for two reasons: the toll returns did not fulfil the company's expectations, and the bridge itself soon proved insufficiently strong to carry the heavy goods traffic which was the expected main source of revenue. It existed for some years as an unprofitable toll-bridge for foot traffic only. Eventually it was taken over by the local authority, who found that the collection of tolls was too expensive an exercise in relation to return and it became a toll-free footbridge, until it was decided that it had to be replaced by the present road bridge. Opened in 1921, having suffered delays in building during the 1914/18 war, today's Southwark Bridge provided a welcome additional crossing for road traffic.

It is a pleasant, wide bridge of steel arches on granite piers and always strikes me as being both clean and spacious. Perhaps this is because it is not so much used by pedestrians as is London Bridge; there is no railway station at either bridge-head to discharge hordes of city workers, and it never appears to be crowded.

Many of London's bridges have some unique feature in their design — on Southwark Bridge, look out for the pier-headings which stand above the parapet; they are in light-coloured stone and are shaped like sentry boxes.

Southwark Bridge provides a route from the south on to Queen Street, off which is Watling Street, a road originally built by the Romans. The other end of the road, if you could follow it every inch of the way, which is not now possible, would take you by the Edgware Road from Marble Arch and thence north by the practical but unromantically-named A5 road, ending on the Island of Anglesey at Holyhead in Wales.

Watling Street may seem to us a strange name for such an important road, but at the London end it really is a narrow street that leads to St Paul's Cathedral. Off it is Bow Lane which has retained its Victorian character; Sir John Betjeman battled to save it from demolition. Bow Lane ends by Bow Church, famous for its bells, at Cheapside; the latter is very much wider in its reconstructed form, the original street having been almost entirely obliterated at the St Paul's end in wartime bombing raids. Queen Street also arrives at Cheapside and continues on the opposite side under the name of King Street, which leads to the City of London Guildhall.

A walk past St Paul's Cathedral will bring you to the top of Ludgate Hill, down which one of the old London gates was sited; at the bottom of the hill, a turn left into New Bridge Street leads to Blackfriars Bridge.

Southwark Bridge

WATERS

BLACKFRIARS BRIDGE

What a pity that another ugly railway bridge obscures the view of this fine bridge from downriver. Even if you are travelling up the river in a boat, the bridges are so close that the eastern side of Blackfriars Bridge can hardly be seen. If the railway bridge, which has nothing at all to commend it in its appearance, had not been placed so close to Blackfriars Road Bridge, the river view looking west would have been really splendid.

The metal work of London's bridges was once mostly painted an uninteresting dull grey colour, of the kind called "battleship grey" or "steel grey". Now the bridges are treated with more attention to their decorative features, using various bright colours in some instances, black and gilt in others.

Blackfriars Bridge is a good example of making the most of designed metal work by the use of light blue and white with special features emphasised in bright red. Behind Blackfriars Bridge stands the railway bridge in the grimy grey paint that was once the standard.

It is a replacement for an earlier bridge; opened in 1869, it is interesting for several reasons. It is the widest bridge on the Thames. It was the first bridge on the Thames to be built using elliptical arches, instead of the rounded Norman type or pointed Gothic type arches of other bridges. It has unique decorative features in the form of pulpits with granite seats built on to each pierhead, an obvious link with the past occupation of the area by monasteries. Its proximity to the now hidden Fleet estuary and the development of the area by the Romans also gives it a more than common interest.

Blackfriars gets its name from the former location there of an abbey which housed an order of Dominican monks who wore black habits. There were many religious orders in the area at much the same time, including a Carmelite order whose inmates wore white habits. Whitefriars Street, just 100 yards or so west of the bridge, near the Temple Inn, reminds us of their past residence there. The Temple Inn nearby is neither a religious establishment nor a hostelry. It is a historic and charming estate of chambers, mainly occupied by members of the legal profession.

Blackfriars history goes back much further than the monasteries. Evidence of Roman occupation and use of the river was confirmed by the discovery of a Roman barge or ship, buried in deep mud, when excavations were made during the building of the road underpass that now goes under the last arch of the bridge, the water having been pushed back by embankment works.

Close to the bridge on the east side stands the famous Mermaid Theatre at Puddle Dock. This dock

was once used by barges and the water lapped round the end wall of the dock warehouse that became the Mermaid. In the small restaurant at the river end of the theatre, you could look down directly at the river flowing below. As a result of the embankment works the river now passes more than one hundred yards away. Just a short way further east stood Baynards Castle. That too had the water lapping its walls but the buried remains of it are now quite remote from the water. The castle was built by Ralph Baynard, a favoured follower of William the Conqueror who gave Baynard the land surrounding the castle site.

It is near Blackfriars Bridge that the River Fleet, which in truth was really a small estuary, flows into the Thames. Nothing can be seen of this Thames tributary except a grid at the bottom of the embankment wall, on the up-river side, which becomes partly uncovered at low tide. Enclosed in a pipe and covered by a roadway, it is one river that has been lost to view with no regrets. It had become a noxious and evil-smelling open sewer through atrocious mis-use.

Trades in London tended in the past to concentrate in particular districts. Around the Fleet, the area was largely occupied by butchers, skinners, leather workers and fishmongers.

The butchers' and fishmongers' stalls were established along the banks of the Fleet and the lower end of the small river that ran into it, the Holbourne. It was common practice for the tradesmen to dispose of offal waste by throwing it into the river. No doubt it was thought that it would in due course find its way out to the sea and make food for the fishes and sea birds. What happened, of course, was that although a certain amount of the waste did get carried out to the sea, some of it was left stranded on the river mud by receding water, to be washed back again by the returning tide. Decomposing waste washing backwards and forwards created a deplorable stench, added to by filth washed by rain from the streets. Both the Fleet and its associated river were suspected of being a major source of disease, and were eventually enclosed.

If you stand at the end of Blackfriars Bridge looking north, you will be looking along New Bridge Street towards Holborn Viaduct, which can be seen to cross the road in the distance, and you will then be looking along the line of the Fleet and the Holbourne River which are now incorporated into the sewer system of London, beneath the roadway.

It is interesting to note that many of the traditional trades areas of London still exist. Although the fishmongers departed to their own market at Billingsgate, near to London Bridge, the butchers remained, moving a little further along to the area adjacent to Holborn Viaduct. London's wholesale meat market of Smithfield is still one of the world's biggest areas of meat distribution.

Holborn Viaduct, carrying a road called High Holborn over what was the "Old Bourne" valley, is worth attention as a quite unusual bridge, being built on brick towers that enclose stairways between the upper and lower levels. Its iron parapets and representative statues mounted on each side of the bridge are further interesting examples of Victorian bridge décor.

Always painted a maroon colour now, with decorative detail picked out by gilding, the design includes winged lions at each end of the bridge, a feature that is included, on a smaller scale, at the bases of the bridge lamps. This bridge, I feel, deserves more attention than it seems to get from the hurrying office workers who daily pass over it.

Anybody particularly interested in Victorian iron architecture would find the central market hall of the nearby Smithfield meat market, especially the roof design, well worth a visit. Be warned, however: the market starts work very early in the day and all is a great hustle and bustle, not at all welcoming to tourists. It is much quieter as midday approaches.

We must return, however, to the river, which up to this point, runs a fairly straight course from Tower Bridge. At Blackfriars, or just a little way upstream, it enters the stretch known as Kings Reach. This is the approach to a bend in the river that almost changes its direction from east-to-west, to north-to-south. Crossing Kings Reach is Waterloo Bridge, the next road bridge up-river, clearly to be seen from Blackfriars Bridge.

WATERLOO BRIDGE

From Blackfriars a dual roadway runs beside the river until it is confronted by the Houses of Parliament buildings at Westminster, after first passing under Waterloo Bridge and another railway bridge.

It is a dual carriageway but not as a result of modern planning for traffic separation, although its construction certainly serves that useful purpose. The double road originated with the coming of electric tramways, when it was divided to take ordinary wheeled traffic on one half, moving in both directions, while the other half was reserved for electrically-driven passenger tramcars. Lines were laid for the double-decked cars with just enough room for those travelling in opposite directions to pass.

There were three rails for each track. The two on the outer edges were for the tram wheels; the third rail, running between the other two, had a different purpose. It had a slot into which a power pickup device, located under the tramcar, was fitted to make an electrical connection. Known as the conduit system, the electrical current conductors ran in a deep channel beneath the slot. These tramlines were a particular hazard for cyclists, especially in frosty or wet weather. The conduit slot was an additional hazard which was not peculiar to all tramway routes. Parts of the track were powered by overhead power lines, but the embankment tramway extended to most routes on the south side of the river.

All tram drivers hated all cyclists for whom not enough room had been left to ride in safety beside the tracks.

With the ending of the tramway system, the Victoria embankment road was made into the present equally-divided dual carriageway.

Whatever method of transport may be available to visitors, I would recommend them to go on foot along this road to Westminster. To stroll easily along under the shade of the plane trees; to watch the river and the ships moored there; and to admire the particularly beautiful dolphin-supported embankment lamps — all this is so enjoyable on a fine day that it is even possible to ignore the roar of traffic on the roadway.

On the way, opposite the lawns of The Temple, you will pass a statuesque image of a dragon mounted on a stone plinth and holding a shield upright. This is the symbol of the City of London, which is repeated at many points of the city boundary. Continuing past the dragon, you will enter the City of Westminster.

Through the line of the embankment lamps and looking across the bows of the white-painted hull of The Wellington (a ship that is now the HQ of the

Master Mariners) Waterloo Bridge can be seen. I remember the long-drawn-out discussions before the war about whether the existing bridge should be replaced with a new one, or whether it was a viable idea to attempt a major renovation of the weakening bridge as it stood.

The first Waterloo Bridge was, another elegant structure designed by Rennie and there was much public support for the idea of preserving it, but it was an impractical idea. An increasing volume of traffic, crossing from the south of London to the Strand and to other developing business areas on the north side, was causing heavy damage and a new bridge was long overdue. As far as cost was concerned, it was estimated that it would be as expensive to keep and rebuild the old one as it would be to demolish it and build a new one.

Built between the years 1811 to 1817, the old bridge had not uncommon foundations based on timber pilings driven into the river clay, to provide a firm setting for the stone piers of the bridge. When the bridge was demolished in 1939 and these piles were hauled out of the clay, it was found that many of them had been preserved by their burial in the clay and were in excellent condition.

Once they had been dried out, the square section timbers were found to be so sound that many of them were split into veneers and used to make decorative furnishing panels. A whole generation of smart new passenger railway coaches of the London, Midland and Scottish Railway Company had their interiors, even in the third class coaches, lined with panels from the timbers that had spent about one hundred and twenty years in the clay below Waterloo Bridge.

In no way does the present Waterloo Bridge look anything like the previous one. For one thing a single arch of the present one spans as much of the river, in graceful elliptical curves, as did two arches of the old one. This gives it an efficient clean look as compared to the yellow york stone balustraded arches of the old. The new Waterloo Bridge is shining white and will probably stay that way now that smoke control regulations are applied to London and coal-burning river craft belong to the past.

Another difference is that the new Waterloo Bridge is free of decorative features. Elegant street lamps were a feature of the old, whereas the new bridge seen from the roadway has a quite utilitarian aspect. Whatever ideas the architect may have had about final decorative touches may perhaps have been abandoned because of the outbreak of war in 1939; certainly, completion of the construction work became a matter of urgency when it became clear, with the approach of the emergency, that labour and materials were going to be in short supply. None of the Thames bridges was ever "taken out" by enemy action, although Waterloo Bridge suffered damage in several of the London air raids. It had been brought into use under conditions of great difficulty, and there was no opportunity for graceful finishing touches. It was enough that the side railings of the footpaths served adequately to prevent people from falling into the river — utility, not architectural merit, was paramount. Viewed from the river, however, the sheer grace of the white arches makes up for what shortcomings there may be above.

Under the last arch on the north side, large doors cover what was once the approach to the Kingsway tramway tunnel. In the days of the old bridge, through the opening that the doors now cover, electric trams used to turn from the embankment road and enter the tunnel into which they barely seemed to fit. Such a manoeuvre today would involve the slow trundling vehicle turning at right angles across two other lines of traffic with the inevitable result of long traffic jams in both directions.

The tramway approach to the tunnel was always a slow one because there was little room in the narrow entrance for the tall, ungainly cars to sway about. From the Victoria embankment they would travel underground to pass under the Strand and Aldwych, surfacing at the top of Kingsway. I was always amused at the sight of these slowly emerging monsters, rising in a railed enclosure protecting the tunnel entrance, like some great marine creature coming up for air. The tunnel is still there although the tramcars are not; during the last war, part of the tunnel was used for safe storage and air raid protection.

Coming across the road or street named The Strand, would you not be looking for some water in justification of the name? In London Strand, you will find a very busy shopping, commercial and theatre street, but it was not always so. It was originally the road which gave access to the river down the steep little roads that lead off it, like Savoy Hill and Villiers Street.

Before the building of the Victoria embankment, these narrow steep roads were the approaches to landing places and quays on the edge of the tideway. The Strand is at a much higher level than is generally realised.

On the north side of the Strand, the streets lead still further uphill into the area of Covent Garden.

In the distant past Covent Garden was a market garden area which became London's main fruit, flower and vegetable market. As a market, it was a

Waterloo Bridge

WATERS

bustling, colourful, congested area, crowded with lorries from all over the country bringing cargoes of fresh produce, and other lorries coming only from London's docks, bearing other goods, particularly fruit, from all over the world.

Where this great variety of flowers and fruit was once sold by the box, basket or sack at auction, there are now arts and crafts shops and fashion boutiques alongside specialist food shops and restaurants. Where the lines of heavy lorries once parked for unloading, tables and chairs are set out upon the cobbles in continental café style, weather permitting.

On one side of the square stands a church known as the "Actors' Church", no doubt because of the proximity of a number of theatres. The church was designed by Inigo Jones, and that famous name associated with it ensures a steady flow of visitors. The world-famous Opera House fronts on Bow Street on the other side of the square.

On the south side of Waterloo Bridge, commonly called "The South Bank", stands the Festival Hall, the Hayward Art Gallery, National Theatre, and National Film Theatre in a neighbourly concrete group. Some people hold that the only benefit of its architecture is that it conceals Waterloo Terminus railway station, but that view of course depends on a person's taste in modern architecture.

HUNGERFORD BRIDGE

Eastwards, the view from Waterloo Bridge is of St Paul's Cathedral standing dominant above Blackfriars, and the pleasant vista of the tree-lined north bank and the ships moored there, giving more opportunities for interesting photographs. Westward, the view is of the heavy mass of Hungerford railway bridge which has as a backdrop the Houses of Parliament.

Close to Waterloo Bridge, moored to the north bank, is the much-admired Scottish paddle steamer "The Old Caledonian". Its career of voyaging round Scotland's lochs and islands ended, it now serves as a floating pub and restaurant. Beyond "Cleopatra's Needle" with its small-scale sphinx guardians there are one or two other ships on this stretch of the river similarly converted.

Along the stretch of the embankment from Waterloo Bridge to Hungerford Bridge and beyond, are attractive public gardens where you can enjoy the fine flower beds, take a snack in the garden café, or, if the mood takes you, be entertained by the open air theatre performances in the summer. You will be sitting or walking on what was once the river tideway, for the whole of the embankment and the gardens are part of the river reclamation scheme that altered the character of the river.

In the far corner of this section of the gardens,

almost under the shadow of the brickwork mass that ends Hungerford Bridge, is the historic watergate. This was a private gateway to the landing stage giving access to the personal river barges for past kings and members of the nobility. As you stand and read the plaque giving details of the watergate, you will be standing on what was the dry landing point. From this you will be able to judge how much of the river was reclaimed, all along the north bank from Blackfriars Bridge, to make the embankment which extends westward to Westminster Bridge and beyond.

Because of its interesting connection with the past, Hungerford Bridge deserves mention where other railway bridges do not.

On a corner of the gardens on the embankment there is a statue of a famous engineer whose work is noted for its wide variety, from under-river tunnels to steamships and many bridges. Is it imagination only that seems to give the face of the statue of Isambard Kingdom Brunel an expression of distaste? Perhaps it is — yet distaste would be justified.

The heavy railway bridge that carries the trains from Waterloo Station on the south side, to Charing Cross station on the north, takes its name from a former bridge that was designed by Brunel and built at this crossing.

It was a beautiful suspension bridge for foot traffic, supported by chain link from towers having a distinct Italianate appearance, which could only have enhanced the view of the river from either up or down stream. When it was decided to allow a railway company to build its bridge on the same line of crossing, the suspension bridge was dismantled although the piers of Brunel's Italian-influenced towers still provide some of the support for the railway bridge and can be easily identified. The chain links were saved and are still in service holding up another bridge designed by Brunel, the famous Clifton suspension bridge that spans the Avon Gorge near Bristol.

The name Hungerford came from a district of that name near to Charing Cross, which was noted for its market. Very much earlier than that it was probably also the point of low tide fording of the river before the embankments were built. Most place names along the river which include the word "ford" indicate the site of an old river crossing.

Foot traffic is still catered for by the present Hungerford Bridge. Steps up from Villiers Street, which leads from the Strand, give access to a footpath which crosses the bridge at the same level as, but separated from, the railway track, to the south bank and Waterloo station.

The walker therefore has a choice of two pleasant ways to reach the next bridge up river — Westminster Bridge. If he stays on the north embankment, he can carry on through more gardens and a promenade beside the river until he reaches Westminster Bridge. If he crosses the footpath on Hungerford Bridge, he will find steps leading down on the south side to a wide riverside tree-shaded promenade, providing agreeable walking westward, past Westminster Bridge and as far as Lambeth Bridge. That, however, is going a shade too far, for there is a great deal of interest at Westminster before we go on to Lambeth.

WESTMINSTER BRIDGE

On the north bank at Westminster Bridge the Victorian embankment comes to an end, blocked by the imposing buildings of the Palace of Westminster, the Houses of Parliament.

Where Westminster Bridge joins the embankment stands a statue group depicting Queen Boadicea of the ancient Britons, charging into battle in a war chariot drawn by bronze horses seeming full of fierce energy. Without doubt the depicted charge was being made against invading Romans, which makes the site of the statue particularly suitable because there is plenty of evidence that the Romans were very active here; many Roman artefacts have been found in the river. In fact, however, this is not the actual spot at which Queen Boadicea led her army against the invader in AD61.

On the opposite south bank, adjoining the bridge, is the building known as County Hall. Built in light stone, with a partly colonnaded facade, and reflected in the water, it looks especially handsome when floodlit, as it usually is at night. Until 1986, it was the seat of London's local government. Changes in the form of local administration decided by Parliament have left the future of the building uncertain. Many Londoners hope that it will survive the change, although demolition to make way for some property developer's scheme may be its fate.

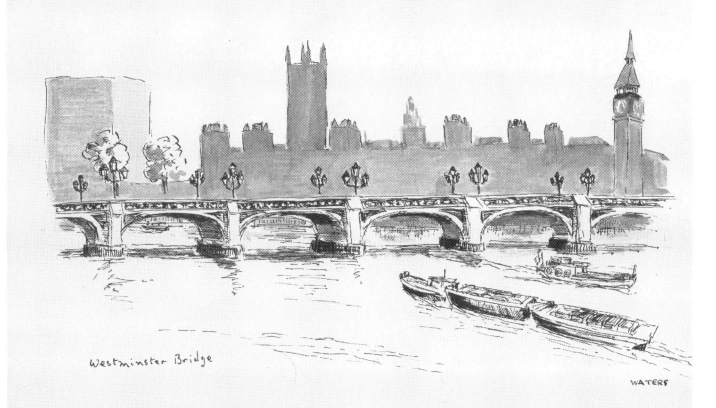

Westminster Bridge

WATERS

Outside the County Hall, on a stone plinth, stands a sculpture of a lion. It was saved from the site of a brewery which was demolished during the post-war south bank redevelopment. It was the brewery company's trademark and a well known Southwark landmark. Westminster Bridge is a decorative, wide replacement for a former bridge which suffered the common distress of tideway bridges. Its foundations were damaged when the old London bridge was removed. The effect of taking away the artificial barrier of the timber round the old bridge piers was to enable the incoming tide to flow much higher upstream; the scouring which this caused made the bridge unsafe. London's rapidly accelerating development also meant that the bridge had become inadequate for the community's needs.

Today's bridge was built wide enough to carry two tramway tracks, now removed, as well as allowing plenty of room for other traffic to flow in both directions. In addition to providing enough space, it has some unique decorative features. Its under-arch decoration, which is flood-lit at night, has not been used on any other bridge. The trefoil design of the parapets and the elegant trios of lanterns for road lighting are unique to Westminster. Originally the lanterns contained several gently hissing gas mantles, giving off a soft yellow light. They have now been converted to electric light but the appearance of the lanterns fortunately remain unaltered.

London was once famous, or infamous, for its thick fogs, which were always particularly dense over the river. I can remember making my way over Westminster Bridge with a hand on the parapet as a guide, in fog that was so dense that I could not see my own feet. The yellow glow from a gas lamp could be only faintly discerned even when one was standing directly underneath. In such fogs, sounds were muffled as if conducted through enclosing cotton wool. The shuffling steps of tram or bus conductors could be heard as they guided the drivers of their vehicles with hand-held flares which could just be distinguished through the fog, although the vehicles that they guided remained almost invisible.

I don't know what effect today's lighting would have in such conditions, because since the passing of clean air acts by Parliament, forbidding the use of smoky fuels for the heating of buildings, such fogs are a thing of the past. The last particularly nasty one, for which the term "smog" — smoke-filled-fog — was invented, was in 1952. That one actually killed prize cattle at an agriculture exhibition being held in London.

A great clean-up of London buildings followed the introduction of legislation. Dark grey buildings were suddenly revealed in their true colour of near white. Carvings and ornamentation of buildings not seen for many years stood out as proud embellishments of grand architecture. During the cleaning of St Paul's Cathedral it was found that the encrustation of soot was up to four inches thick in some places.

Westminster Bridge is a good place from which to look downstream and appreciate the attractiveness of a clean London where once all was grey and grimy. There is much activity on the river at this point associated with Westminster Pier, where pleasure boats may be boarded for trips up or down river. There is a constant coming and going of patrol launches of the Thames Division of the London Metropolitan Police force, and of commercial vessels.

LAMBETH BRIDGE

Lambeth Bridge marks the point of another historic river crossing. Along the north bank, the route is past the Houses of Parliament, with the Palace of Westminster buildings on one side of the road and Westminster Abbey and St Margaret's Church on the other. Public gardens, entered just past the tall Victoria Tower at the end of the Parliament buildings, allow you to come in contact with the river again quite close to Lambeth Bridge. For the best distant view from the south side of the Houses of Parliament walk down the steps at the end of Westminster Bridge to the pleasant promenade that leads to Lambeth Bridge.

This bridge replaces not only an earlier suspension footbridge but also a much older bridge and an earlier ferry crossing. Other Thames ferries were in the form of boats rowed by watermen for foot passengers. The Lambeth ferry was different. It was known as the "Horse Ferry". It was in the form of a flat, raft-like craft, designed to carry horses and carriage, together with passengers.

From the north end of Lambeth Bridge, where a traffic roundabout smooths out the cross-flow of traffic with Millbank, a road, still called Horseferry Road, once terminated at the river bank. The other end of the road was convenient to St James's Park and Buckingham Palace. It was a direct way to South

London via the ferry that avoided the longer drive along the Strand, through Ludgate and over the congested London Bridge.

The ferry was within the keeping of the Archbishop of Canterbury whose Palace is situated on the south bank close to the present Lambeth Bridge. At this crossing, the ferrymen were servants of the Archbishop and the tolls collected went to his estate as revenue to pay for the upkeep of the ferry and the wages of the ferrymen; no doubt there was something left over to go into the general coffers.

Crossing by the Horseferry was a hazardous business and horses and vehicles using it were apt to be dumped in the water well short of the bank for which the ferry was aiming. A public demand for a bridge at that point arose when King James I had to be rescued from a most unpleasant ducking when the ferry failed to reach the shore. He was probably lucky to escape with his life. Because the ferry revenue was part of the Archbishop's income, the request for a bridge was strongly resisted by the church and of course by the ferrymen who stood to lose their livelihood.

What may have finally persuaded the church that a bridge was desirable was the increasing number of mishaps resulting in passengers and their coach and horses failing to complete the crossing without get-

ting wet. Oliver Cromwell, who no doubt had some strong words to say about horse ferries, was saved from such an accident by the skin of his teeth.

Eventually a wooden bridge for foot traffic only was built and this was replaced in 1862 by a suspension bridge, also for foot traffic, which was itself replaced by the present road bridge in 1932.

When this bridge was being built, my work sometimes took me across the river from Lambeth to Victoria. I usually walked across a temporary footbridge that had been provided while the new road bridge construction went on. Like most members of the public I was curious to see how the work was progressing but was frustrated in this by tall wooden board panels that completely screened the building operation from view. For some reason the builders of large projects seem to find it necessary to keep their activities secret from the public. How much more interest is now created by the provision of viewing points on large sites, so that the progress of the work can be seen.

Opened in 1932 by King George V, the new Lambeth Bridge certainly eased traffic congestion on Westminster and on the next bridge up stream, Vauxhall Bridge. The considerable increase in traffic since then makes it difficult to realise what a benefit the new bridge was. Perhaps we need another now

Lambeth Bridge

to relieve the traffic congestion on Lambeth Bridge.

At each end of the bridge there are gilded finials like huge pineapples topping tall stone columns. When the bridge was first built, the roadway lighting was not really adequate, the lamp standards being too far apart to give good illumination. This was put right when square trellis-like pylons were added to mark the jubilee of King George V. Originally painted white, these pylons looked an obvious addition and seemed quite out of style with the rest of the bridge. In today's livery however, painted black, they seem much more acceptable.

Standing on the down-stream side of the bridge, there is more opportunity for photography and sketching; the Houses of Parliament and their riverside terrace on one side, and Westminster Bridge ahead, provide plenty of scope for interesting pictures. Lambeth Palace, the London home of the Archbishop of Canterbury, is to the right, but not much more than the gatehouse can be seen from the bridge.

Standing on the up-stream side, the view is towards Vauxhall. On the left, the Albert Embankment leads past the headquarters of London's Fire Brigade. A floating landing-stage in front of this building provides mooring for a floating fire brigade station and its fire tenders, somewhat like river tugs with hose monitors mounted on them.

On the opposite side of the river there is Millbank, probably so named because at one time there were water mills on that part of the river. The area was the scene of disastrous flooding in 1928. Millbank and the area where the tower office block now stands, and bounded by the Horseferry Road for some distance back, received a considerable volume of flood water. Worse damage and more loss of life was caused further up river near to Putney Bridge by the same flood tide. After this disaster the embankment wall was raised at Millbank, which is why only a tall person walking beside the river at this point can get a reasonable view of it.

London is said to be slowly sinking and many fears have been expressed in the past about the risk of further floods in spite of the raising of the height of the embankment. The matter was debated off and on for some five decades before positive action was taken to cope with the threat of extra high tides, driven by strong east winds, meeting high volume rainwater flood from the upper Thames.

In 1983 a system of retractable flood barrier gates built across the river below Woolwich, known as the Woolwich Barrage, was brought into use. Its effectiveness was tested a few months after its completion when it held back a large volume of potential flood water from reaching London.

Either embankment, the Albert on the south side or the Millbank on the north, provides a good riverside walk to Vauxhall Bridge. For those who choose the north bank and wish to rest from river scenes, the Tate Gallery, near Vauxhall Bridge, which the road passes, provides a notable collection of paintings and sculpture.

VAUXHALL BRIDGE

Where Vauxhall Bridge links its banks, the river again begins a change of direction back to east/west. The district of Vauxhall on the south bank was once the site of the famous Vauxhall Pleasure Park; Vauxhall Walk, Glasshouse Walk, and the Lambeth Walk — which enjoyed some fame in a song from a theatrical show of the 1930s — are reminders of where the gardens once were. There was nothing of glamour, though, about the Lambeth Walk in 1938. The extensive estates of slum cottages were already being replaced by new blocks of flats before air-raids forced the pace of demolition a couple of years later.

In their heyday the walks were pleasant tree-lined promenades frequented by members of fashionable society. Similar pleasure gardens were also developed at Chelsea on the other side of the river, such as the equally famous Ranelagh Gardens and the Cremorne Gardens.

In the time of King Charles II, from Vauxhall westwards the river ran through what were then healthy rural areas, its banks lined by flower- and vegetable-growing market gardens and fruit orchards. It is difficult to visualise it now as you stand looking westwards at the industrial aspect that is the view from Vauxhall Bridge.

The down-stream view towards Lambeth Bridge, with its background of the Parliament buildings, is pleasant enough but there is no tranquillity here. A constant stream of traffic pours over the bridge from Victoria to South London, while northbound vehicles peel off on to the bridge from a complex one-way traffic system on the south side, all in noisy contrast with the placidly flowing water below.

The first Vauxhall Bridge was built in 1816 and was the first iron bridge across the Thames. The present one built between 1895-1906 is another example of Victorian designers' flair for decoration. Not that the bridge seen from the roadway has anything about its appearance to commend it. Its functional design, however, is relieved by symbolic statues on each of the arch supports. They depict various crafts and industries, and activities such as engineering, architecture, agriculture, fine art, local government, science, education and pottery. The figures stand with their backs to the bridge and unfortunately can only be seen well from a boat.

A little over forty years after the opening of the bridge, the Vauxhall Gardens, to which the bridge gave convenient access, closed. From that moment the district rapidly deteriorated into an overcrowded slum of small dwellings.

Because of the change in the direction of the river it is not possible from the bridge to view the scene very far upstream.

The south side is occupied by a heliport, industrial buildings and wharves. This is the area still known as Nine Elms which was once a quiet little village, so named because there were nine elm trees along its high street. The many crumbling industrial buildings which had replaced the cottages of Nine Elms have also disappeared in their turn to make way for London's new wholesale fruit and vegetable market, which retains the name Covent Garden Market from its previous location near the Strand. There are other wholesale produce markets in London but Covent Garden of today is the largest and unlike the former market is not open to the public.

Vauxhall Bridge

WATERS

CHELSEA BRIDGE

Heading west from Vauxhall Bridge on the north bank, you will soon find that a tree-lined promenade gives a good view of the river once again and of the industrial development on the other side.

Directly opposite stands Battersea Power Station. Not now producing power, its function having been taken over by more modern generating stations, it stands as an example of what was considered to be outstanding industrial design of the 1930s. Nobody quite knows what to do with such a structure but many people feel that it is worth preserving, and no doubt a suitable plan for its use will emerge. It now looks forlorn, with no vapours rising from its massive but not overpowering chimneys. They were once proudly flood-lit at night, looking shining white with clouds of vapour and smoke pouring out of them giving an impression of the powerful activity within. It was a most impressive sight against the dark backdrop of the hill behind Battersea and a foreground of broken light reflections in the flowing river water.

I liked to see the coal ships — for it was a solid-fuel fire station — manoeuvre across the river to tie up at the unloading wharfs. These ships were a special kind of collier, built with very little super-structure so that they could pass under London's bridges. The river men referred to them as flat-irons.

When empty they would rise high on the water so that as they returned downstream towards the sea, the top half of their screws thrashed out of the water. They could only navigate downstream near half tide, because without a cargo they were too tall to pass under the bridges at any higher tide level.

The north bank of the river continues as a tree-lined walk from this point through historic riverside scenery up to Battersea Bridge, three more bridges on.

Before reaching Chelsea Bridge, another railway bridge is passed, the Grosvenor Bridge, giving multi-track railway access to the Victoria Station terminus, from the south coast and southern suburbs of London. Its name comes from the Grosvenor family who once owned most of the land around the Victoria district. One thing to remark about the Grosvenor Bridge is that it is really three bridges each built close beside the other. The second and third were added to enlarge the traffic-carrying capacity of the first bridge, as the demand increased from travellers on the Southern Railway line between Victoria and Brighton on the south coast. The journey time between these two points fifty years ago was advertised as fifty minutes. Now it takes longer.

The later bridges were of course built at different times with the expectation that each addition would

Chelsea Bridge

prove to be adequate, and less costly than building an entirely new bridge. The result is another unattractive mass which on the downstream side hides from view the functional though still attractive Chelsea suspension bridge, which replaces a much more decorative one.

Viewed from a position on the west or upstream side, the former old Chelsea Bridge seemed to be related to the next one, the Albert Bridge, which has been saved from redevelopment. Both the old bridges were of similar design and spanned the river to approach what is now the Battersea Park. This stretch of the river, with its tree-shaded Chelsea embankment on the one side and the Battersea Park promenade on the other, is very pleasant indeed.

The original Chelsea Bridge was completed the year before the opening of Battersea Park, which was constructed after the closing of Vauxhall Gardens in 1859.

When the new bridge was being built, I travelled daily along the Chelsea Embankment and was interested to note the progress of the work. A difference in design was immediately apparent in that the new bridge had higher and plainer supporting towers than those used on the old. As work progressed to the cable-laying stage another important difference became apparent. The old bridge was supported by large flat-link chain-like suspension arms held together by large nuts and bolts. Steel rods of different lengths held the bridge span to the links which were attached to the suspension arches. For the present bridge, flexible wire cables have been used. These were laid singly by the use of a high crane and a cable-carrying cradle. Many steel cables were laid on each side in this way and were clamped together after laying.

While the first parts of the bridge were being built outward on pilings from each shore and the towers and cables were being put into place, the middle sections were being built on barges moored to the embankment wall of Battersea Park. I was intrigued to see the work going on over there and wondered about its purpose. I found out eventually, when there appeared to be two ends of a bridge jutting out from opposite banks and cables hanging in a sweeping ark across the river with no middle part. It transpired that the parts being constructed on the barges could be placed in position only on one particular day, when an exceptionally high tide would occur. Work scheduled on this part of the construction, in fact, was determined not as usual by time, but by tide.

At the appropriate moment, tugs hauled the barges carrying their bridge sections to a position up river and then carefully steered them down on a falling tide to align them with the shore construction. There they held them steady, and as the tide ebbed and the barges lowered, the bridge sections settled onto jacks that had been prepared to receive them. A first class piece of planning and workmanship.

Cables attached and painting completed, the bridge opened in 1937. It was a larger bridge than the one it replaced, without the old style of decoration. At night the plainness is masked by chains of light bulbs that etch the bridge outline and its carrying cables against the sky and then it no longer looks so hard and functional.

Chelsea Bridge is by no means the first to be built using pre-fabricated sections. A variation of the technique was used in the building of the world's first iron bridge across the Severn Gorge in Shropshire, from which the town of Ironbridge took its name.

The Iron Bridge is a single hundred-foot span and a particular interesting feature of it is the way in which it was designed. Although it is built of cast iron parts, the designer must have been a carpenter, because dovetail and mortice joints and wedges have been made in iron and used in the construction as if the material used had been timber.

But Iron Bridge had no problem of strong tidal water to contend with such as there is at Chelsea and the method of using the ebbing tide was what made the Chelsea Bridge project so fascinating. Even so, it was not the first time that the tide was used in bridge building on the Thames. For a bridge much further upstream, at Barnes, a variation of this technique was employed.

From Chelsea Bridge there are two very pleasant ways to reach the next bridge up river, the decorative Albert Bridge.

There is the opportunity for a pleasant stroll along the river frontage of Battersea Park on the south side, which is well away from the noise of traffic. On the north or Chelsea side there is also a fine embankment walk which passes the Albert Bridge. Road traffic on this route is heavy and noisy but this might perhaps be compensated for by the historic interest of the area. Directly across the road, enclosed by railings, are the lawns of the Chelsea Hospital, home of the famous military Chelsea pensioners. Once a year the lawns become covered by a town of canvas show tents and beautiful gardens, each constructed in a matter of a few days, for the world-famous Chelsea Flower Show.

In one part of the grounds are the ancient "physic gardens". Here were grown the herbs used by London's apothecaries as the ingredients for their medicines and ointments. Chelsea was considered to be a particularly healthy and curative area, and was a great source of fruits, vegetables and flowers in the days of Henry VIII. Many famous persons built grand houses there, including Henry.

ALBERT BRIDGE

Innumerable places were named in a spirit of patriotic enthusiasm for the sovereign in the 19th century: buildings, railway stations, parks, streets and public houses. Albert Bridge, of course, was named after Queen Victoria's consort, Prince Albert.

It is a typically Victorian period suspension bridge for which the London public has a great affection. It looks very attractive in the bright paint colours that have been chosen to show its decorative iron work to advantage, although some may think that pastel tints are inappropriate for an iron bridge. I have heard it remarked that it looks rather like a decoration for a birthday cake, but most people would agree that it is more pleasing to the eye than when painted in the old drab grey colour. It is a very similar design to that of the old Chelsea Bridge and together they make a very picturesque pair.

Like so many of the Thames bridges, it became weakened by heavily increasing traffic as larger goods vehicles came into use; at one time it was threatened with demolition but was saved by the even heavier weight of public protest. In agreeing to spare it the authorities were faced with the problem of what to do about making this old and ailing bridge safe.

For a while it was closed to all wheel traffic and then the rather incongruous pillars were placed

Albert
Bridge

A

WATERS

under the centre of the bridge to give it added strength. Odd though it may seem to prop up the middle of a suspension bridge, it was clearly a very practical solution and we still have a graceful but fully working example of Victorian suspension bridge building that seems "just right" for the area.

Onward from Albert Bridge the walk leads to the next bridge upstream which can be seen from the Albert Bridge. On the other side of the road is Cheyne Walk, which before the embankment was built ran close beside the river.

Cheyne Walk has many associations with King Charles II, it being much in favour as a fashionable place in his day. There are still many charming period houses which, like the old church which stand prominently at one end of the walk, owe their serene appearance to the skill of restorers after suffering damage from bombing raids during the last war.

At the north end of the Albert Bridge stands the David Wynne statue "Dolphin and Boy", which is the pair to the one seen at Tower Bridge and is another admirable example of the sculptor's work.

BATTERSEA BRIDGE

At the end of Cheyne Walk is Battersea Bridge, which like so many of the tideway bridges is a replacement of a much earlier one. On the other side of the river is the old village of Battersea, which is difficult to identify now since it has long been absorbed into the London urban sprawl. St Mary's, a fine old church with a river frontage and an old inn standing behind it, probably identifies the centre of what was at one time a separate small community some miles out from the City of London.

At Battersea the ground level is higher than that on the opposite north bank and this caused the river at this point to be wide and shallow until it was confined by embankment. There is some evidence that the Romans forded the river at this point in a running fight with the Britons. Many items of Roman arms and armour have been discovered in the river mud near this point at what must have been a fording place.

Today's bridge runs on a straight line across the river, quite unlike the old one which changed its line as it went. It was a simple timber structure and was the subject of a famous painting by Whistler, showing river craft alongside the bridge timbers and a background of the river bank, and giving a good idea of the rural nature of the river in his day. William Turner also found the old bridge to be an attractive

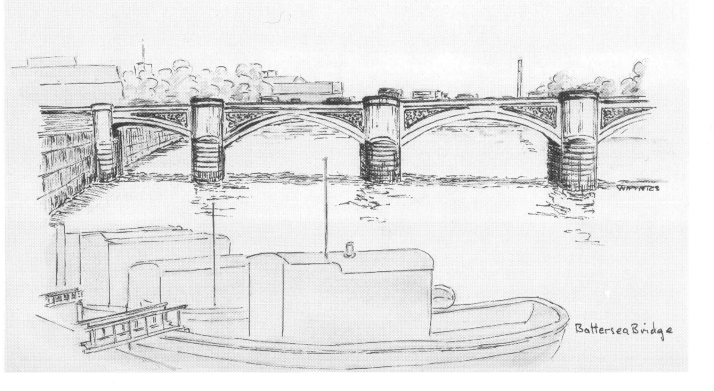

Battersea Bridge

subject and painted it several times, and many famous artists have lived in the surrounding district of Chelsea.

From the middle of the bridge, looking downstream towards Albert Bridge, the tree-lined banks on each side still hold something of their nineteenth century aspect. On the other side of the bridge, when the traffic pauses to give you an opportunity to cross the road, the upstream view in complete contrast is with one exception an industrial scene. A power station provided power for London's underground railway system is prominent on the right bank. Factories and warehouses line the river on the opposite side.

The one sight that is strangely alien to this scene is the Chelsea Reach houseboat moorings that huddle close to the bridge. A collection of houseboats and small craft linked together by duck board pathways makes this into a floating village and is unique on the Thames Tideway. The houseboats are at rented moorings, have electric power supplied to them and have a recognised postal address.

Many yards of photographic film have been shot at this glorious neighbourly huddle of boats by professional and amateur photographers, and many are the paintings and sketches that have been produced of this surprising and strangely attractive use of the river.

Beyond Chelsea Reach the road curves away from the river behind the dark mass of the Lots Road Power Station, the warehouses and dingy streets where once the Cremorne Pleasure Gardens were laid. A rather forlorn little notice beside a bridge in the Kings Road marks the place where the wrought iron Cremorne Gates guarded the entrance to riverside gardens.

Wandsworth Bridge

WATERS

WANDSWORTH BRIDGE

From Battersea Bridge nothing can be seen of the river from the roads going on westwards, because of industrial developments, until the approach to Putney Bridge.

In between comes another railway bridge and also Wandsworth Bridge, the latter an unremarkable working bridge of no particular merit other than that it is a strong wide span of steel and is adequate for the job that it has to do. Only students of bridge building will find it worth making a detour to examine this bridge, the river aspect from which in both directions is industrial. Opened in 1937, Wandsworth Bridge is of girder construction and is a departure from the style of other Thames bridges, replacing an earlier one built in 1873.

The first bridge at Wandsworth suffered from the same problem that bedevilled nearly all the early London bridges, which had to be replaced or widened because of the overwhelming increase in the volume of traffic. The earlier Wandsworth Bridge, by all accounts, was a shoddy piece of work and was made subject to a weight limitation order. There are no such restraints on the present bridge.

PUTNEY BRIDGE

To arrive at Putney Bridge, follow the Kings Road into New Kings Road and then to its end at Fulham High Street, where a turn left past the church will lead you onto the bridge. The river traveller, carrying on upstream after passing under Wandsworth Bridge, first approaches another iron railway bridge which also has provision for foot traffic.

I know this area quite well as I lived near Putney Bridge as a boy. It was a bit of an adventure to climb up the steps to the footpath of the "Iron Bridge", as it was locally known, and stand in the middle of it and wait for a train to arrive. The old Iron Bridge would, and probably still does, rattle and shake with foot-penetrating vibrations whenever a train passed, and this was thought to be good fun.

This was the area that was stricken with disaster in 1928, the year the floods came.

Close to the bridge were blocks of flats, a tennis court and the Hurlingham Club. When the river overflowed, the whole of this area became inundated with flood water which washed up into part of Fulham, flooding the surrounding roads for a distance of about half a mile. Unfortunately, the lower flats of the building were below ground level and quickly filled up with water. Rescue services could not reach the people trapped in these flats and those that could not escape by swimming out of the windows were drowned. It was to prevent a recurrence of such flooding, which also occurred in Millbank on the same night, that the Thames barrage, already referred to, was built.

As for Putney Bridge, we have again the familiar story that it is a replacement of an older bridge, but it differs from the usual story in that when the present bridge was built the name was also changed. The original bridge at this point was a simple wooden bridge called Fulham Bridge, Fulham being the district on the north side, opposite Putney on the south side.

On each end of Putney Bridge stands a church; the two were almost identical in appearance until a bad fire seriously damaged St Mary's on the Putney side. All Saints Church on the Fulham side, for which I have a special affection, because that was the church of my marriage, stands on the edge of a fine park, called "Bishops Park", because it was once part of the grounds of the Bishop of London's Palace. The latter building is now an educational establishment.

Putney Bridge spans the river on roughly the same line as the old Fulham Bridge. Originally it was quite narrow and when electric trams were a popular mode of public transport it carried two tram tracks over the same space as that used by other traffic. Riding across on a bicycle, which I often did, was a rather tricky business. Hard granite cobbles between the curbstone and the inside tramway line left a space of rather less than twelve inches to ride in. We learned to ride straight in those days or were brought down by skids on lines or cobbles, especially when they were wet with rain.

The bridge was widened in 1930 by almost as much as its original width. Tram-lines were removed as the tall narrow tramcars became outmoded and were replaced with the short-lived pneumatic-tyred trolley buses. The main benefit of this was the replacement of granite cobbles with a first-class macadam surface.

Mention Putney Bridge to most Londoners and ask what it is best known for, and the response will probably be "That's where the boat race starts". Indeed that is so. The annual race up the Thames between crews of eight from the Oxford and Cambridge universities is started from a position just above Putney Bridge. When I was a lad the event was one that really involved people locally, whether or not they had any direct connection with the University towns. They took sides, wearing the pale blue or dark blue colours of the crew that they favoured.

For about two weeks before the day of the race the scene was one of carnival along "Putney Towpath", as the south bank of the river is called.

People came to watch the crews bring their boats out from the famous boathouse and embark on their training sessions on the water.

There was plenty more to watch in those days, too: numerous street entertainers, musicians, tumblers, escapologists, hucksters and sellers of badges and rosettes. They filled the roadway so that it was hardly possible for a vehicle to get by because of the crowds that surrounded each performer.

On the day of the boat race great crowds gathered on the towpath and filled the riverside walk of Bishops Park opposite. Putney Bridge was a grandstand densely lined with people watching the preparations of the start.

Behind the starting posts was gathered a small armada of launches and passenger river-craft of all sizes that were set to follow the crews along the four-and-a-half mile course. When they all moved off, a respectful distance behind the rowing crews, the wash they caused always overwhelmed the bank on the Putney side and front row spectators invariably suffered wet feet, without seeming to care.

Today, the boat race — nobody now calls it the "Oxford and Cambridge Boat Race" — is still a popular event though there is no longer the atmosphere of carnival nor are the crowds as dense as

those that once gathered at Putney Bridge to witness it.

Putney lies at the bottom of the "U" bend that starts at Battersea and continues as the river's course takes a sweep up towards Hammersmith, where the direction again changes with the start of another "U" bend in reverse.

It is generally considered to be important for a boat race crew to be leading at Hammersmith Bridge, which is just out of sight from Putney and where they can take advantage of the river's change of direction.

I spent much of my leisure time near this part of the river and was always fascinated with the interesting movement of tugs and other river craft. Two things in particular pleased me immensely. One of these was the sight of a tug with a string of laden barges in tow. Sometimes one tug would have six or seven barges lashed behind. A Thames tug had tall funnels that were pulled down, on approach to a bridge, by a member of the crew hauling on a line that was attached near the top of the funnel. In the horizontal position it could pass under the bridge at high tide. If it happened that you were looking over the parapet of the bridge as a tug passed under, you got a quick glimpse of the base of the smoke-stack before a cloud of dark, soot-laden smoke caused you

Putney Bridge

WATERS

to withdraw your head in a hurry. A smell like the inside of a railway tunnel filled your nostrils.

The other thing which I enjoyed was the sight of an unladen barge, or lighter as they are also called, being taken down-stream on an ebb tide. They have no engine or sail and could be manned by a single oarsman. When empty the lighters sit high on the water. The oarsman stood at one side of the vessel at the stern end and held onto a very long sweep in a rowlock. He would walk forward several paces raising the sweep from the water as he did so. Then, lifting the end high so that the blade dipped in the water, he would walk, pushing against the sweep, and then repeat the movement, with extraordinary slow grace. His skill was such that he could steer his large empty craft under bridges and round bends, using his knowledge of the current.

I have not seen this done for many years now, and the coal-burning tugs have given way to diminutive diesel-engined vessels that look like floating tractors. They seem to be powerful enough to do the work of the old tugs but have none of the character of the larger craft.

Putney towpath becomes a gravelled riverside footpath that passes under Hammersmith Bridge and emerges on the road to Barnes. The alternative road routes are along Fulham Palace Road and through Hammersmith Broadway, or across Putney and Barnes Commons and through the village of Barnes.

HAMMERSMITH BRIDGE

Across the bend of the river at Hammersmith is hung — I think that is the right word — a suspension bridge of the same ornate kind as Albert Bridge. It is almost a copy of the first suspension bridge that was built across the Thames at this point sixty years earlier.

New embankments to shape the river's curving course and to control low ground flooding made it necessary to rebuild, although the form of the first bridge was closely followed. What we have today is a beautiful bridge which, if it were appraised on the grounds of efficiency only, would be replaced. I am sure that any proposal to replace it would produce the same storm of public protest that saved the Albert Bridge. People love a graceful bridge across water. Too narrow it may be, and it is no doubt frustrating to heavy goods drivers since it can take only a limited amount of weight. Moreover, it shakes and vibrates at the passing of buses and it frequently needs re-painting. Like the Albert Bridge, it is a relic. Yet nobody who will spare the time to walk across it and look at it from the river would want it changed.

Hammersmith is an important stage in the boat race which ensures that each year a large crowd gathers on the bridge to watch the race crews "shoot" under it, and to make an assessment of which will be the probable winner.

From here on the riverside is taking on an increasingly suburban, in some parts almost rural, appearance. Industry is being left behind and trees and meadows more frequently become the green edge to the river. Some light industrial activity appears here and there to give a most interesting mix to the river scenery. On the north side, the road runs straighter than the river, which veers away from it and is difficult to follow. On the south side, the road follows the river curve fairly closely and once past water reservoirs it is again in contact with the river near to the old village of Barnes. To reach Barnes from the north bank, cross Hammersmith Bridge and turn right at the traffic lights. Walkers can join the riverside footpath by turning down towards the river on the *left* side of the bridge and passing under it. This is the footpath from Putney which joins the road to Barnes.

By old Barnes village the river again starts on another "U" bend. The road runs close to the water and opposite, across the river, is the Duke's Meadows which we shall visit after inspecting the next road bridge upstream. But before that there is Barnes Railway Bridge.

Two interesting points about the railway bridge are worth mention. One is that the trellis-type steel sections of which the bridge is constructed were prefabricated and brought along on barges to be placed on its stone piers, making use of the receding tide. This was a similar technique in a smaller way to that used in the construction of the Chelsea Bridge. The other point is that the public footpath that is provided by this bridge had to be specially strengthened to take the very large number of people who crowd onto it to watch the university boat race crews "shoot" this last bridge on the race course.

After passing under the road arch of Barnes Bridge the road again leaves the river and arrives in about half a miles at Mortlake village and then, by a serpentine route to the right, at a very busy traffic crossroads. In fact five roads meet at this point, one of which, the fourth right, leads to Chiswick Bridge.

CHISWICK BRIDGE

Chiswick Bridge was built to provide a river crossing for the A316 road to the Upper Richmond Road to the A4 link with the motorway route going westwards out of London.

That the bridge does its work of relieving traffic congestion on the alternative routes no doubt gives satisfaction to its designers, but from the roadway it is often unrecognised as a bridge.

Seen from the river, however, it has a clean and graceful appearance. The centre arch has a span of over one hundred and fifty feet which is the longest concrete span of any Thames bridge. A riverside view is worth a detour from the end of the bridge.

You must watch for the second turning on the right as you leave the bridge going towards Chiswick. A signpost points the way into a small turning which leads to Duke's Meadows. It is an uninteresting but short stretch of road which, after passing a few houses, runs alongside some railed allotment gardens and leads you into the riverside terrace of Duke's Meadows with its very convenient and ample car parking space.

The old village of Barnes is directly across the river from the terrace and the small river-craft and rowing activity in its foreground make a restful scene.

Chiswick Bridge, which is still close at hand, cannot be seen from the meadows because it is screened by the Barnes railway bridge and the curve of the river. The riverside road can be followed through, cautiously, because it is really a narrow and winding lane that passes behind boathouses. When the tide is low there is at this point quite a stretch of shingle shore uncovered at the bottom of the concrete slopes that lead down from boathouses.

The whole area is open to free public use. Good picnicking space is provided all along the bank as far as Chiswick Bridge and it is on this part of the river, west of Barnes railway bridge, that the university boatrace course comes to an end. Motor traffic is slowed as it travels along this lane by humps or "sleeping policemen" laid across its width. From the picnic area the white Chiswick Bridge can be seen to advantage and appreciated for the fine bridge that it is.

Follow the narrow lane and it will lead you back to the main road after passing under a low archway on a right-angle bend.

Near to the end of Chiswick Bridge, traffic lights control the crossing from this lane into one on the opposite side of the main road and you will then be on your way to Strand-on-the-Green and Kew Bridge.

STRAND-ON-THE-GREEN and KEW BRIDGE

Strand-on-the-Green, once a busy riverside village, is today a surprising haven of peace surrounded by constant hustle and bustle. At least, it would have been totally surrounded but for the river frontage that saved it, and the fact that all motor traffic is prohibited. The charming houses and cottages on the river front are all that remain of the village of Strand-on-the-Green. Cars can be street-parked nearby.

Its name indicates that it was at one time an important point of river transport, Strand in this context being the road giving access to the river by goods transport, thus providing a convenient way of sending to London the produce for which the area was noted. The "Green" part is undoubtedly Kew Green on the other side of the river.

To the north of Kew is the M4 motorway and the very much older Great West Road, which was built in the 1920s through plum and apple orchards and was expected to be London's once-and-for-all-time exit to the West. Its successor, the M4 motorway, already notorious for its traffic jams, seems to have been only partly more successful than the Great West Road in providing a free-flowing traffic route at this point.

Fortunately none of the hustle and bustle and roar of traffic reaches Strand-on-the-Green. Its bay-

Chiswick Bridge

WATERS

windowed cottages, carefully maintained by proud owners, are a delight. The riverside view of trees, cottages and the buff stone Kew Bridge makes it easy to forget that it is all part of a London suburb. Even the tall railway bridge carrying suburban train services across the river does not do anything to spoil the charm of the area, which provides more scope for camera and sketchbook.

The footpath through Strand-on-the-Green connects with a road at the end of Kew Bridge which runs through Brentford and Hounslow. At one time it crossed Hounslow Heath, long since developed out of existence, which was a notorious area in the past for the operations of highway robbers and footpads. Brentford, as its name indicates, was the location of another old fording place.

Across Kew Bridge is Kew Green, a preserved area that has managed to escape the progress of bricks, mortar and tarred macadam. The result is an area of surprisingly rural appearance, with the bridge and old inns providing a most attractive place to linger for a while.

It is a pity that the gas holder at Brentford and the tall blocks of flats standing behind it have ruined the view of the mellow stone Kew Bridge with its prominent Coat-of-Arms on its centre arch when seen from Strand-on-the-Green. From Kew Green, however, the worst of modern development does not intrude.

On the opposite side of the road a wide tree-lined green also gives access to the world-famous Royal Botanical Gardens. Kew Gardens, as they are commonly called, cover a considerable area beside the river from Kew Bridge towards Richmond, and are full of interest at any time of the year. A whole day spent there might leave you a little foot-weary but never bored unless you dislike plants, trees and shrubs, exotic greenhouses and peaceful open spaces laid out to please the eye as well as to educate. There are museums to visit and the great tropical hot-house with its steaming jungle heat, set beside a lake where fat carp swim.

Kew Bridge is built in Purbeck stone, which is generally described as white but has mellowed by time. It has an ideal setting in Kew Green.

Except for travellers by boat the river disappears from view to run between the meadows of Kew Gardens and Syon Park, but is only a short journey by road to the historic town of Richmond-upon-Thames.

Kew Bridge

RICHMOND LOCK

At Richmond there are two road bridges, one foot bridge and a railway bridge.

Richmond Bridge is an antique. It is the oldest bridge on the tideway and is in the centre of the famous royal town of Richmond. Before proceeding into the town, however, it is interesting to turn aside at the roundabout traffic approach to it and take the road which passes the old deer park and crosses the river towards Twickenham by the more modern bridge, which although in the Borough of Richmond is known as Twickenham Bridge.

If you cruised up the river from Kew in a passenger boat, before arriving at Richmond you would first approach Richmond Lock with its unique Victorian footbridge and half-tide retractable dam.

The footbridge can also be seen to be quite close to Twickenham Bridge on the downstream side. To reach it from the road, if you are travelling by car, it is necessary to cross Twickenham Bridge, carry on to the first traffic roundabout, double back on your tracks and turn off left as you again approach the bridge. I have found that it is usually possible to park a car somewhere on the road beside the river.

The unusual design of bridge that connects with the Richmond lock on the other side of the river is an old toll footbridge, which is now free of tolls.

On the south side of this attractive and picturesque area there are wide green meadows which in winter are regularly flooded from river overflow, but which always recover to their lush green natural pasture. The north side is built up as a street of large and handsome houses set well back from the riverside, so that together with the trees that screen them they add to, rather than detract from, the environment.

Under the footbridge walks are suspended steel dams that are drawn up clear of the water at high tide so that river craft can pass under the arches. When the water is low, however, the dams are lowered in order to retain water in the upper river. Navigation is then only possible by passing through the lock on the Surrey side which is the first lock on the tideway.

This bridge was built as a result of local protest when the old London Bridge was demolished and it was found that this affected the flow of the river, which was reduced at low tide to a small stream running between stretches of grey mud. The presence of the bridge acts as a dam, holding back much of the water until the tide returns.

The road bridge at this point, Twickenham Bridge, is a young one opened in 1933 to relieve the pressure of an increasing flow of traffic to the westward routes. It looks like a stone bridge but it is really

TWICKENHAM BRIDGE

stone-clad concrete. Engineers will no doubt find it interesting that the piers rest on a footing of compressed cork.

It is not far to walk into Richmond Town from Twickenham Bridge. Even if you are travelling by car for which you have been fortunate enough to find a parking space near the river, I recommend the walk. Car parking in the town of Richmond is not easy, even to those who know the town well.

If you follow the river, within sight of the town you will pass under a tall railway bridge, and onto a footpath separated from the water's edge only by a strip of grass. This of all of the Thames railway bridges is the least displeasing.

At Richmond the river is very much alive with pleasure craft of all kinds: hired rowing boats, self-drive motor boats, sailing dinghies, cabin cruisers and larger fare-paying passenger craft. Humped over all this activity, with a background of Richmond Hill and its planted terraces, is the white stone Richmond Bridge.

It was built between the years 1774/77 and was originally a toll bridge, about two-thirds of the present width. When it was found necessary to widen it, the upstream side was dismantled and the piers extended so that the extra road width would be added. All of the removed stone was carefully stored and

RICHMOND BRIDGE

replaced in its original order. If you look under the bridge arches today you will see the difference in colour of the under-arch stonework which indicates the extent of the bridge widening.

It is a bridge of a design that is unique on the river but neither it nor the congested narrow streets of Richmond could have coped with the increasing volume of traffic, from which it has been relieved by Twickenham Bridge. But for the building of that bridge, Richmond Bridge and no doubt some of the town's ancient buildings would necessarily have been demolished.

The view of the river from the top of Richmond Hill has been a famous subject for many artists and the walk up there is well worth while for the sake of the view and for a look at the royal Richmond Park, which is entered through gates at the top.

Within the town itself, between the greens and the river front, are the old buildings of Richmond Palace, approached by the quiet lanes surrounding them. Onwards from Richmond towards the top of the tideway at Teddington the north bank footpath follows the river through the historic Marble Hill Park, to join with a lane to Twickenham old village.

It may seem strange that Twickenham is further up river than Richmond while the bridge that bears its name is slightly down river. This is most probably

Twickenham Bridge

because the bridge is on a route that bypasses Richmond town, although still within its borough boundary, and leads towards Twickenham.

At Twickenham the last bridge on the tideway before the locks at Teddington links the old village of Twickenham with Eel Pie Island. It is a quaint-looking part hoop of a footbridge spanning a quiet backwater of the river, the main tideway passing on the other side of the island.

Eel Pie Island gets its name because of its shape, which is that of an old-fashioned traditional style of eel pie, at one time a favoured local dish. Although there are no more bridges before Teddington the journey up river to that point is very pleasant and it is a pity that when travelling by road only rare glimpses of the river can be seen. It is best appreciated on this stretch from some small gardens on the left in what is known as the Strawberry Vale area.

It is not far from Twickenham to Teddington by road.

If you leave the narrow old streets of the riverside you will emerge into an unremarkable suburban shopping centre. The turn to take is left at the traffic lights; in less than two miles, where another set of traffic lights marks the junction of a road beside an unusually tall church, the narrow road on the left leads in short distance to the river and locks.

Parking may be difficult because busy television studios are located near-by and it may be necessary for a motorist to drive round the secondary road to find a parking spot where the car may be safely left.

The walk back, which would probably not be far, will be well rewarded by the extraordinarily cluttered river view of small craft, several locks, the lock weir and the foot suspension bridge which gives access to it.

We have now reached the top of the tideway but for those who wish to travel still farther, there is a most enjoyable and interesting time ahead, through the lovely Thames valley. Those retracing their steps back through London will perhaps be surprised to discover how different the river looks when travelling down stream.

Only those with unlimited time will be able to do more than touch the outer skin of the intricate and fascinating history of the river and its environs, but those who have the opportunity to study the river Thames still further will derive infinite interest and pleasure from doing so.

Richmond Bridge

WATERS

Bridge to Eel Pie Island

Teddington footbridge

WATERS

UNDER-RIVER CROSSINGS

An alternative to crossing the river by bridge is to burrow under it. There are a number of tunnels bored under the Thames but those that can be used by members of the public independently are all across the lower reaches of the river, east of Tower Bridge. Those crossing above Tower Bridge, west, toward Teddington, are all railway tunnels. London's railway systems developed on the north (the city) side and trains to and from the south were all carried across the river on bridges. It was the need for the London Underground rail system to reach southern suburbs that brought tunnels into use.

The first attempt was the tunnel designed and built by Marc Brunel on a line almost the same as that of Tower Bridge. It was intended as a railway tunnel but its building was fraught with trouble and never came into use.

There are now four tunnels to carry the Underground "Tube" trains, crossing the river from Vauxhall Bridge (the Victoria line being just west of it) and London Bridge, and a short line route that connects the mainline Waterloo station, on the south side, with the centre of the city on the north.

Road and foot tunnels cross at several points below Tower Bridge. The first, another design by Marc Brunel, was completed years behind schedule after many mishaps and is still in use today, connecting the Underground rail system from Whitechapel to New Cross. Known as the Thames tunnel it is the world's first under-river tunnel and was completed in 1868. A road tunnel from Wapping to Rotherhithe, a very busy traffic route, was opened in 1908. An earlier one still further east between Blackwall and Greenwich was opened in 1897 and is still in use, supplemented by a second tunnel linked to it, built to cater for greatly increased traffic flow, opened in 1966.

Shortly after the Blackwall tunnel was finished, a project for a foot passenger sub-way between Poplar and Greenwich was started. It was opened in 1902, and the most easterly tunnel of all is another subway for foot traffic, between the Isle of Dogs and Woolwich, opened in 1912. All of these crossings, with the exception of the Brunel tunnel close to Tower Bridge, are still in use.

Further downstream is Dartford Road Tunnel which was opened in 1963, almost a mile long and has two tunnels.

BRIDGE STATISTICS

TOWER BRIDGE	opened 1894	800ft between towers — road bascules each weigh about 1,000 tons — cross the river about 30ft above high tide.
LONDON BRIDGE	opened 1973	three spans — 800ft long — 105ft wide.
SOUTHWARK BRIDGE	opened 1921	five arches — 517ft long — 55ft wide.
BLACKFRIARS BRIDGE	opened 1869	five arches — 923ft long — 105ft wide.
WATERLOO BRIDGE	opened 1942	five arches — 1,230ft long — 80ft wide.
WESTMINSTER BRIDGE	opened 1862	seven arches — 827ft long — 80ft wide.
LAMBETH BRIDGE	opened 1932	five arches — 776ft long — 85ft wide.
VAUXHALL BRIDGE	opened 1906	five arches — 809ft long — 80ft wide.
CHELSEA BRIDGE	opened 1937	suspension — centre section 300ft long — 83ft wide.
ALBERT BRIDGE	opened 1873	suspension — total length 710ft — 41ft wide.
BATTERSEA BRIDGE	opened 1890	five arches — 413ft long — 55ft wide.
WANDSWORTH BRIDGE	opened 1940	three steel spans — 664ft long — 60ft wide.

PUTNEY BRIDGE	opened 1886 (widened 1932)	five arches — 664ft long — 43ft wide. to 83ft wide.
HAMMERSMITH BRIDGE	opened 1887	suspension — centre section 688ft long — total length 822ft — carriageway 27ft wide.
CHISWICK BRIDGE	opened 1933	three river arches — 450ft long plus shore arches — 70ft wide.
KEW BRIDGE	opened 1903	three arches — 1,182ft long — 55ft wide.
RICHMOND LOCK	opened 1894	298ft long. A footbridge across river and barge lock — two walkways 9ft wide — 16ft apart — space between, houses half-tide dams retracted. Barge lock — 280ft long — 37ft wide.
TWICKENHAM BRIDGE	opened 1933	three arches — 1,235ft long — 70ft wide.
RICHMOND BRIDGE	opened 1777 (widened 1937)	five arches — 300ft long — 24ft wide. to 36ft wide.
EEL PIE ISLAND BRIDGE		a small footbridge crossing from old Twickenham village to the island — does not cross main river.
TEDDINGTON WEIR BRIDGE		suspension footbridge giving access to the locks and weir from the Middlesex side.

BRIDGES FOR ROAD TRAFFIC
(all have footpaths)

	Years of Building		Designer
TOWER BRIDGE		1886-94	Sir Horace Jones
LONDON BRIDGE	1st Stone Bridge 1204		
	2nd	1825-31	John Rennie
	Present	1967-72	Lord Holford (Architectural Adviser)
SOUTHWARK BRIDGE	1st	1814-19	John Rennie
	Present	1912-21	Sir Ernest George
BLACKFRIARS BRIDGE	1st	1760-9	Robert Mylne
	Present	1860-9	Joseph Cubitt and H Carr
WATERLOO BRIDGE	1st	1811-17	John Rennie
	Present	1937-42	Sir Giles Gilbert
WESTMINSTER BRIDGE	1st	1738-1750	Charles Labelye
	Present	1854-62	Sir Charles Barry (Architectural Consultant)
LAMBETH BRIDGE	1st	1861	P W Barlow
	Present	1929-32	Sir Charles George Humphreys
VAUXHALL	1st	1811-1816	John Rennie
	Present	1895-1906	Sir Alexander Binnie
CHELSEA BRIDGE	1st	1851-8	Thomas Page
	Present	1934	
ALBERT BRIDGE		1871-3	R M Ordish
BATTERSEA BRIDGE	1st	1771-2	Henry Holland
	Present	1886-90	Sir Joseph Bazalgette

WANDSWORTH	1st	1870-3	J H Tolmé
	Present	1936-40	Sir T Pierson Frank
PUTNEY BRIDGE	1st	1727-9(Timber)	Sir Joseph Alworth
	Present	1882-6	Sir Joseph Bazalgette
	Overhauled	1973-6	
CHISWICK BRIDGE		1933	Sir Herbert Baker
KEW BRIDGE	1st	1758-9(Timber)	John Barnard
	2nd	1784-9(Stone)	James Paine
	Present	1903	Sir John Wolfe-Barry and Cuthbert Brereton
TWICKENHAM BRIDGE		1933	Maxwell Ayrton
RICHMOND BRIDGE		1774-7	James Paine
	Widened	1937	

BRIDGES FOR RAIL (r) OR RAIL AND FOOTWAY (f)

Cannon Street (r) — 1863-6 for South Eastern Railway

Blackfriars (r) — 1862-4 Western Bridge for London and Chatham and Dover Railway — disused
1884-6 Eastern Bridge

Hungerford or Charing Cross (r/f) — 1864 for South Eastern Railway

Grosvenor or Victoria (r) — 1858-60 Eastern Side for L.C.D.R.
1865-6 Western Side for London Brighton and South Coast Railway

Nine Elms (r) — 1863 for London and Southampton Railway

Putney (r/f) — 1887-9 for London and South Western Railway

Barnes (r/f) — 1846-9 for London and South Western Railway — disused
1891-5 alongside downstream

Strand-on-the-Green (Kew) (r) — 1864-9 for London and South Western Railway

Richmond (r) — 1st bridge 1848 for Windsor Staines and South Western Railway
2nd bridge 1908

FOOT BRIDGES ONLY

Richmond Lock   Eel Pie Island   Teddington Lock

Other Books available from Pryor Publications

"Buy a fine Singing Bird?"

Old London Street Cries

A quality reprint of an 1885 edition of Old London Street Cries with over 140 pages of informative and interesting reading together with over 50 woodcuts depicting various street traders of London from the seventeenth century.

This hard back book is hand bound with marbled paper and unusual book ties, it also has hand coloured frontispiece.

The book measures approximately five inches by four inches.

London's City Recorder — "Beautifully Illustrated"   **Price £6.75 inc. Postage**

Don't:
A Manual of Mistakes & Improperties more or less prevalent in Conduct & Speech.

DON'T, a best seller of the early 1880s, is a reflection of a society long since past and makes interesting and amusing reading now.

This is a copy of the original measuring 4½" x 5½" and contains such diverse advice as:

DON'T say "hung" when "hanged" is meant. Men, unfortunately, are sometimes hanged; pictures are hung.

DON'T say "lady" when you mean wife.

DON'T be servile towards superiors.

DON'T wear diamonds in the morning.

Price £2.75 inc. Postage

Old London Bridge

An eye witness account of the laying of the first stone of John Rennie's bridge in 1825.

Illustrations of the bridge in various stages of construction and of the previous bridge first built in 1208 add further interest.

There is a short summary of the history of the bridge from its opening in 1831 to its re-erection in the Arizona desert in 1968.

Price £1.00 inc. Postage

IN PREPARATION

Tunnels under the Thames
St Katherine's Dock

Bibliography and Other Thames Reading

Title	Author
THAMES CROSSINGS	Geoffry Phillips
LONDONS RIVERS	Philip Howard
LONDONS RIVERSIDE	Susanne Ebel and Doreen Impey
PORTRAIT OF LONDONS RIVER	Basil E Cracknell
THE CHANGING RIVER	Anthony Burton
A VIEW OF THE THAMES	Norman Shrapnel
THE FACE OF LONDON	Harold P Clunn
THE LONDON ENCYCLOPAEDIA	*Editors* Ben Weinred and Christopher Hubbert
LONDON UNDER LONDON	Richard Trench and Elis Hillman